I0018288

Page Formatting

Easy Word Essentials
Volume 2

M.L. HUMPHREY

TITLES BY M.L. HUMPHREY

CONTENTS

INTRODUCTION

In *Word for Beginners* I covered the basics of working in Word and in *Intermediate Word* I covered more intermediate-level topics. But I realized that some users will just want to know about a specific topic and not buy a guide that covers a variety of other topics that aren't of interest to them.

So this series of guides is meant to address that need. Each guide in the series covers one specific topic such as formatting, tables, or track changes.

I'm going to assume in these guides that you have a basic understanding of how to navigate Word, although each guide does include an Appendix with a brief discussion of basic terminology to make sure that we're on the same page.

The guides are written using Word 2013, which should be similar enough for most users of Word to follow, but anyone using a version of Word prior to Word 2007 probably won't be able to use them effectively.

Also, keep in mind that the content in these guides is drawn from *Word for Beginners* and *Intermediate Word*, so if you think you'll end up buying all of these guides you're probably better off just buying *Word for Beginners* and *Intermediate Word* instead.

Having said all of that, let's talk page formatting, including how to add page numbering, headers, and footers to your document.

BREAKS

Before we talk about numbering your document or adding a header or footer to your document, it's important to understand how to insert breaks in your document and what those do. There are three main types of breaks: page breaks, column breaks, and section breaks.

PAGE BREAKS

When I think of page breaks, I think of stopping where I am on the current page and moving to the top of the next page. For example, I use page breaks at the end of all of my chapters in my ebooks.

The simplest way to insert one is with Ctrl + Return. Or you can go to the Insert tab and click on Page Break under the Pages section. Or, last but not least, and the one I tend to use, you can go to the Page Layout tab, click on Breaks, and then select Page (the first option) from the dropdown menu.

For all three options, you should have your cursor positioned at the point in the document where you want the break to appear, so directly after your last sentence in that section.

(One thing to note: Sometimes Word is strange and when you insert a break at the end of a sentence it will stretch out the last line of text as if trying to justify it. To get rid of this, just go to the end of that sentence and hit enter once. That should return the last line to normal spacing.)

COLUMN BREAKS

A column break allows you to make sure that text you want in a specific column appears in that column. To insert a column break, click into the document at the point where you want the new column to start and then go to the Breaks dropdown menu in the Page Setup section of the Page Layout tab and select Column from the dropdown menu. This is only relevant when you're using multiple columns, otherwise it behaves like a page break.

SECTION BREAKS

Section breaks are essential for when you want to change the header or footer between parts of your document or for when you want to use a different page orientation or number of columns in different parts of your document. For example, I use section breaks in all of my print books to separate the title page, etc. from the main chapters in the book. I also use them when I have blank pages at the end of a chapter in a non-fiction book that I need to be completely blank. In a business or school setting, you could use section breaks to separate an appendix from a report, for example.

The section break I use is the Next Page option. It's the first one listed under Section breaks and it inserts a break and starts a new section at the top of the next page.

To insert it, do just like you would with a page break. Go to the point in the document where you want the break, go to the Page Setup section of the Page Layout tab, click on the dropdown for Breaks, and choose Next Page.

As you can see in that dropdown, you can also insert a section break in the middle of a page using the continuous section break option. You could use that option for a document where you want to use multiple columns on only one part of the page or where you want the text across columns to split before reaching the bottom of the page. (For example, a page with two separate articles where article A is the first half of the page and article B is the second half of the page.)

You can also set section breaks so that not only do they move to the next page, they move to the next even or odd page. This would be ideal for formatting my non-fiction books, for example, where I want all chapters to start on odd-numbered pages. However, I tried using it in a book I was formatting and it did not work well for me at all. At first it looked great. It inserted a completely blank page for the even-numbered pages at the end of a chapter (which is what I wanted) and started the next chapter on an odd-numbered page. But I then noticed that when I inserted the next section break the one I had already inserted reverted back to a simple section break that just started on the next available page. So I can't recommend (at least in Word 2013) using the odd and even page section break options unless you only have one in your entire document.

(What can I say? I'm brilliant at breaking things other people think work.)

So those are the three types of breaks. Think of a section break as allowing you to create completely separate documents within a single Word file, each of which can be formatted differently. Next, let's talk about page numbering, headers, footers, and page orientation.

PAGE FORMATTING

Page formatting is most relevant when it comes time to print your document. The key issues to consider for page formatting are page numbering, headers, footers, and page orientation.

HEADERS AND FOOTERS

If you want text to repeat at the top or bottom of every page, then you should use headers and footers. Do not try to manually put this information into your document. One little change to your text and it'll break. (Not to mention how it'll look on an ereader.)

A header goes at the top of your page.

A footer goes at the bottom of your page.

To add one, go to the Header & Footer section of the Insert tab and click on the arrow below the one you need (header or footer), and then choose the option that works best for you.

You're not stuck with the format you choose. For example, with short story submissions, they usually want the header to be in the top right corner. If you choose the Blank header option, that creates a header that's in the top left corner. But you can simply go to the Home tab and choose to right-align the text in your header and that will put it in the right corner instead.

After you choose your header or footer option, Word inserts [Type here] into the designated spots where you're supposed to put text. To edit this text, just start typing because it will already be highlighted in gray. If it isn't, select the text and then start typing. Text in your header or footer works just like text in your document. You can use the same options from the Home tab to change your font, font size, color, etc.

Headers and footers are in a separate area from the main text of your document. So if you're in a header or footer and want to go back to the main document, you can (1) click on Close Header and Footer in the menu bar, (2) hit the Esc key on your keyboard, or (3) double-click on the main text in your document which will be grayed out while you're in the header or footer.

If you're in your main document and want to open a header or footer, you can (1) double-click on the text in the header or footer, or (2) right-click on the header or footer and choose "Edit Header" or "Edit Footer" from the dropdown options. I've found in recent versions of Word that double-clicking when there's just a page number in the footer doesn't work well for me and that I have to right-click and choose Edit Footer instead. This was not true of older versions of Word.

BASIC PAGE NUMBERING

Any page numbering you add to your document should be added as part of the header or footer. DO NOT manually add page numbers to your document. Word will do this for you and by letting Word do this, you ensure that the page numbering isn't changed when you make edits to the document.

To add page numbers to your document, go to the Header & Footer section of the Insert tab and click on the arrow next to Page Number. This will bring up a dropdown menu that lets you choose where on the page you want your page numbers and then how you want those page numbers to look.

That should be all you need. Go there, choose Bottom of Page, Plain Number 2, and you'll have a document that has a page number centered at the bottom of each page.

DIFFERENT FIRST PAGE
HEADER/FOOTER/PAGE NUMBER

If you open most books you'll see that there isn't a header on the first page of any chapter. It's blank. But then the rest of the chapter does have a header. And if you have a report with a cover page, chances are you won't want a header on that cover page. So how do you do this?

First, insert a header. Now, look at the menu bar above your document. You should see a Design tab with the label Header & Footer Tools. Like this:

Options for First and Odd/Even Pages

If you look in the center of that tab, you'll see a section called Options and a box labeled Different First Page. If you check the box, Word will treat the first page of any section differently from the other pages in the section.

Be careful when using this one, because if you're on the first page of the section, that header you enter is only going to show on that page. If you're on a different page of the section and you make edits to the header, they won't be reflected on the first page. So always be sure to check your headers on ALL pages when you're done.

Also, at least in my version of Word, making that choice applies to both the header and footer. So I had a document with text in the header and page numbering in the footer. When I chose "different first page" for the header section that also removed my page numbering from that first page. I had to open the footer and choose Page Number under the Header & Footer Tools to put a page number on that first page.

And don't worry if it takes a few tries to get your headers and footers looking the way you want them to. I've been doing this for years and I still make mistakes. Remember Ctrl + Z (Undo) is your friend.

Also, with a really complex document that has lots of different sections and headers/footers, I would save a version before you start, just in case. Sometimes it's easier to start over rather than try to undo everything you've done wrong.

DIFFERENT ODD AND EVEN PAGES

I don't recall ever using this with a business report or school paper, but I do use it with book formatting. Pick up a book from your shelf and you're liable to see that most books have the title or current chapter name on one page and the author name on the facing page throughout the main body of the book.

How do you do this?

First, insert your header or footer. Next, click on Different Odd & Even Pages in the Options section of the Header & Footer Tools Design tab. Similar to how it worked above, once you make that choice, any changes you make to an odd-numbered page will only apply to your odd-numbered pages and any changes you make to an even-numbered page will only apply to your even-numbered pages.

It gets really fun when you have both the Different First Page box checked and the Different Odd & Even Pages box checked, because that means you have three separate headers and footers per section.

If you're going to be doing this a lot, it's a good idea to build a template that you can work with each time. (For example, for paperback formatting KDP provides templates with sample text. If you ever use Word to format a book, I'd highly recommend using them.)

HEADERS AND FOOTERS AND SECTION BREAKS

The choices we just discussed allow for some pretty sophisticated formatting without ever requiring a section break. But if you have any blank pages in your document (say between chapters or sections) or if you need to have different headers or footers (say in an appendix), then you're going to need to combine the use of section breaks with the use of headers and footers.

We already talked about how to insert a section break. That's very simple. (Page Layout tab, Breaks dropdown menu.) And the nice thing about Word is that it defaults to continuing your page numbering as well as your headers and footers across sections.

If you look in the Headers & Footers Tools Design tab you'll see a Link to Previous option that is already selected by default. This means that, unless you do something to change it, your header and footer in this section are going to be the same as your header and footer in your surrounding sections.

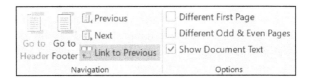

So, if for example you inserted a section break to start a new chapter, then you likely don't have to do anything else. Word will treat the first page of that new chapter the same as it did the first page of the last chapter and will keep the header and footer settings and contents you had set for that prior section.

If, however, you insert a section break because you want to change something in the header or footer compared to the sections around it, then you're going to need to unlink the section before you make your changes. Otherwise, you will change all sections in your document at the same time. For example, when I insert a section break to create a blank page on an even-numbered page at the end of a chapter, I make sure the Link to Previous option is no longer selected before I delete the page number at the bottom of the page.

It's a best practice to always scroll up and down about three pages when you make an edit like this to make sure you didn't delete the header or footer on another page. It's amazing how easy it is to delete something on page five and also delete something on page eight. (Remember, in any given section you could have three different headers and footers, so a change you make on page five may not affect the headers and footers on pages six and seven, but could still affect the headers and footers on page eight.)

ADDING DATE AND/OR TIME TO YOUR HEADER OR FOOTER

This one is actually pretty simple. To insert the date and/or time into your header or footer, go to the location where you want to insert it (the header or footer), and then go to the Header & Footer Tools Design tab. In the Insert section click on Date & Time. This will bring up a Date & Time dialogue box. Choose the date and/or time format you want.

If you want the date and time to update so that it always displays the current time, be sure to check the box that says so. (Just be sure that's what you really want. I can't count the number of memos I've seen where someone used the automatic date option and shouldn't have. Instead of the memo being dated the day it was actually written and finalized, the memo updated to the current date each time it was opened. That may not seem like a big issue, but if you're writing a memo to a file to document when an important event occurred it can become a very, very big issue.)

ADDING DOCUMENT INFORMATION TO YOUR HEADER OR FOOTER

You can also have the header or footer include certain document information such as the Author, File Name, File Path, or Document Title.

To do this, navigate to where you want this information to be (the header or footer), and then go to the Header & Footer Tools Design tab and click on the dropdown for Document Info in the Insert section. You can choose Author, File Name, File Type, and Document Title from the dropdown menu. If you want to include other information about the document, click on Field in the dropdown menu. That will open a dialogue box with a number of options to choose from.

All of the document information fields are dynamic fields, so will update as the information changes.

EDITING HEADER/FOOTER POSITION OR FONT

By default in Word 2013, the header and footer are positioned .5" from the top and bottom of the page. If you want to change that setting, it's in the Position section of the Header & Footer Tools Design tab.

To change the font, font size, or color of the text in your header or footer, it works just like normal text formatting. Select the text you want to change and use the options in the Font section of the Home tab. You can also select the text you want to change and then right-click and pull up the Font dialogue box.

MARGINS

Margins are the white space along the edges of your document. The default in my version of Word is one-inch margins all around which is what most submission guidelines I've seen require, so you usually won't need to edit these. But in case you do...

(Because it looks like at least in Word 2003 the margins were not one inch all around.)

Go to the Page Layout tab and under the Page Setup section click on the dropdown under Margins. You will see some standard choices to choose from or the option at the bottom to set custom margins. If you click on Custom

Margins, it will take you to the Page Setup dialogue box where you can specify the margins for top, bottom, left, and right.

You can also open the Page Setup dialogue box directly by clicking on the expansion arrow for the Page Setup section.

PAGE ORIENTATION

A standard document has a page orientation of portrait. That's where the long edge of the document is along the sides and the short edge is across the bottom and top. This is how most books, business reports, and school papers are formatted, and it's the default in Word.

But sometimes you'll create a document where you need to turn the text ninety degrees so that the long edge is at the top and bottom and the short edge is on the sides. A lot of tables in appendices are done this way. And presentation slides are often this way. That's called landscape orientation.

(Think paintings here. A drawing of a person—a portrait—is taller than it is wide. A drawing of a mountain range—a landscape—is wider than it is tall.)

To change the orientation of your document, go to the Page Setup section of the Page Layout tab, click on the arrow under Orientation, and choose the orientation you want.

(If you use section breaks you can set the page orientation on a section-by-section basis. But if you're not using sections changing the orientation on any page will change the orientation of the entire document.)

FOOTNOTES AND ENDNOTES

You can also add footnotes or endnotes to a document. Footnotes go at the bottom of the page. Endnotes go at the end of the document or the section. Other than that, they're pretty similar in how they work and how you insert them into your document.

To insert a footnote or endnote, position your cursor at the location in the document where you want to place it and go to the Footnotes section of the References tab. Click on either Insert Footnote or Insert Endnote. Here's an example of a footnote that I inserted into a document:

> As you may have noticed, I like to make side comments a lot. I usually do them in parens within the text of the document, but another way to handle that would be to insert a footnote or endnote.[i]
>
> ---
> [i] *Like this one.*

See how it's separated from the main text of the document by a short line and then numbered with a superscript number 1 and how there is also a superscript number one in the main body text to indicate what the footnote is referring to?

The default is for the text of the footnote to be in the same font as the main body text but in a slightly smaller

(10 point versus 11 point) font size. If you want to change that, you can change the style of the footnote or you can simply edit the footnote like you would normal text. (Unlike headers and footers, you don't have to double-click to access a footnote or endnote.) If you edit it like normal text, select the text and then use the options in the Font section of the Home tab or right-click and open the Font dialogue box.

If you want to change the style of your footnote, you can right-click on the footnote and choose Style from the dropdown menu. This will bring up a Style box that includes a basic summary of the font and font size, etc. that are used for footnotes. Click on Modify and that will bring you to the standard Modify Style dialogue box where you can change the style for all of your footnotes at once.

What you see above is the standard appearance and format for a footnote. If you want more control over your footnotes and/or endnotes, you can click on the expansion arrow in the bottom right corner of the Footnotes section of the References tab to bring up the Footnote and Endnote dialogue box. This allows you to change where the footnotes and endnotes display as well as how they're numbered. This is also where you can choose to convert your footnotes to endnotes or vice versa.

(To convert an individual footnote or endnote to the other option, you can right-click on that specific footnote or endnote and choose the Convert To [X] option from the dropdown menu.)

If you need to delete a footnote or endnote, you have to do so in the document itself. Deleting the text of the footnote or endnote will still leave the number in your document. Selecting and deleting the small superscripted number in your text will delete both the number and the contents of the footnote/endnote.

Be careful if you have footnotes or endnotes in your document and you're copying and pasting sections or changing the font or font size that you don't also change the font and font size for the numbering of the footnotes and endnotes. I know this can happen in older versions of Word, although I wasn't able to replicate it in Word 2013 when I tried to do so.

If you have track changes turned on and you edit the text in an endnote or footnote, those edits will show in track changes. However, you cannot tie a comment to an endnote or a footnote. The best you can do is put the comment close to the location of the endnote or footnote. Also, when you're reading a document, if you want to see what the text of a footnote or endnote is without going to the end of the page or end of the section or document, you can do so by holding your cursor over the number of the footnote or endnote.

CONCLUSION

So that's the basics of page formatting in Word.
    If you get stuck, reach out at:

mlhumphreywriter@gmail.com

I'm happy to help. I don't check that email account every single day but I do check it regularly and will try to find you the answer if I don't know it.
    Good luck with it!

APPENDIX A: BASIC TERMINOLOGY

TAB

I refer to the menu choices at the top of the screen (File, Home, Insert, Design, Page Layout, References, Mailings, Review, View, Developer) as tabs. If you click on one you'll see that the way it's highlighted sort of looks like an old-time filing system.

CLICK

If I tell you to click on something, that means to use your mouse (or trackpad) to move the arrow on the screen over to a specific location and left-click or right-click on the option. (See the next definition for the difference between left-click and right-click).

If you left-click, this selects the item. If you right-click, this generally creates a dropdown list of options to choose from. If I don't tell you which to do, left- or right-click, then left-click.

LEFT-CLICK/RIGHT-CLICK

If you look at your mouse or your trackpad, you generally have two flat buttons to press. One is on the left side, one is on the right. If I say left-click that means to press down on the button on the left. If I say right-click that means press down on the button on the right.

Now, as I sadly learned when I had to upgrade computers and ended up with an HP Envy, not all track pads have the left- and right-hand buttons. In that case, you'll basically want to press on either the bottom left-hand side of the track pad or the bottom right-hand side of the trackpad. Since you're working blind it may take a little trial and error to get the option you want working. (Or is that just me?)

SELECT OR HIGHLIGHT

If I tell you to select text, that means to left-click at the end of the text you want to select, hold that left-click, and move your cursor to the other end of the text you want to select.

Another option is to use the Shift key. Go to one end of the text you want to select. Hold down the shift key and use the arrow keys to move to the other end of the text you want to select. If you arrow up or down, that will select an entire row at a time.

With both methods, which side of the text you start on doesn't matter. You can start at the end and go to the beginning or start at the beginning and go to the end. Just start at one end or the other of the text you want to select.

The text you've selected will then be highlighted in gray.

If you need to select text that isn't touching you can do this by selecting your first section of text and then holding down the Ctrl key and selecting your second section of text using your mouse. (You can't arrow to the second section of text or you'll lose your already selected text.)

DROPDOWN MENU

If you right-click in a Word document, you will see what I'm going to refer to as a dropdown menu. (Sometimes it will actually drop upward if you're towards the bottom of the document.)

A dropdown menu provides you a list of choices to select from.

There are also dropdown menus available for some of the options listed under the tabs at the top of the screen. For example, if you go to the Home tab, you'll see small arrows below or next to some of the options, like the numbered list option in the paragraph section. If you click on those arrows, you'll see that there are multiple choices you can choose from listed on a dropdown menu.

DIALOGUE BOX

Dialogue boxes are pop-up boxes that cover specialized settings. As just mentioned, if you click on an expansion arrow, it will often open a dialogue box that contains more choices than are visible in that section. When you right-click in a Word document and choose Font, Paragraph, or Hyperlink that also opens dialogue boxes.

Dialogue boxes allow the most granular level of control over an option. For example, the Paragraph Dialogue Box has more options available than in the Paragraph section of the Home tab.

(This may not apply to you, but be aware that if you have more than one Word document open and open a dialogue box in one of those documents, you may not be able to move to the other documents you have open until you close the dialogue box.)

CONTROL SHORTCUTS

I'll occasionally mention control shortcuts that you can use to perform tasks. When I reference them I'll do so by writing it as Ctrl + a capital letter. To use the shortcut just hold down the control key while typing the letter specified. Even though the letter will be capitalized, you don't need to use the capitalized version for the shortcut to work. For example, holding down the Ctrl key and the s key at the same time will save your document. I'll write this as Ctrl + S.

ABOUT THE AUTHOR

M.L. Humphrey is a former stockbroker with a degree in Economics from Stanford and an MBA from Wharton who has spent close to twenty years as a regulator and consultant in the financial services industry.

You can reach M.L. at mlhumphreywriter@gmail.com or at mlhumphrey.com.

www.ingramcontent.com/pod-product-compliance
Lightning Source LLC
LaVergne TN
LVHW052126070326
832902LV00038B/3964

If you want to print a document from Word, chances are you'll need to know how to format that document including adding headers, footers, and page numbering.

This guide covers that as well as page and section breaks and more.

ISBN 978-1-950902-26-2
50799